The Essence of Southern Royalty.

# The Essence of Southern Royalty.

## Bolling Heard Brown III

### Contribution by Waunience Cole Brown

XULON PRESS

Xulon Press
2301 Lucien Way #415
Maitland, FL 32751
407.339.4217
www.xulonpress.com

Unless otherwise indicated, Scripture quotations taken from the King James Version (KJV) – *public domain*.

Printed in the United States of America

Paperback ISBN-13: 978-1-6628-4052-4

# THE
# ESSENCE
# OF
# SOUTHERN
# ROYALTY.

# Table of Contents

# Bolling Heard Brown III
## United States Marine Corps
## 1977-1990
## in Dress blue uniform

Bolling joined the United States Marine Corps in 1977 and was honorably discharged in 1990 under medical conditions with full medical and retirement benefits. During his illustrious Marine Corps career, he was combat ready, trained with weapons, explosives, and martial arts, as well as in office administration. He also trained at the Coronado Naval Seal Training Academy Base in San Diego, California, where he still lives with his family today. He also was highly decorated for all of his honorable services; his highest award being a Navy Unit Commendation medal citation. He still tells everyone who asks him of his military career, that he would not be here today if it were not for his belief in God, faith, constant belief in prayer, and everlasting guidance to do the right things in God's eyes.

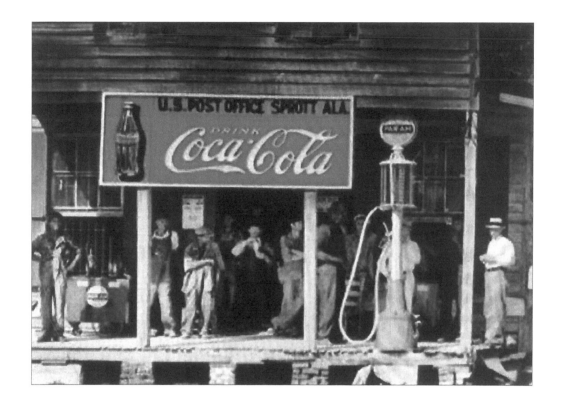

Country store in Sprott, Alabama, where my late brother, James Clarence Brown Jr., was believed to be on the front porch of the store after a hard day's work. He also marched with the great Dr. Martin Luther King Jr. from Selma to Montgomery.

This is my true story.

I was born on September 28, 1958 in a small, rural town called Sprott in the state of Alabama to Mrs. Annie Ruth Heard Brown and Mr. James Clarence Brown. We lived on a fifteen acre farm that was built by my dad and family. The house had four bedrooms with a huge fireplace in the parlor room and two bathrooms. We grew our own food and it was always plentiful, as I recall. We grew every kind of vegetable that you could think of: tomatoes, potatoes, corn, beans, and hot peppers. Also on the farm were chickens, horses, dogs, and cows.

From left to right-
First Cousin: Bruce Herald Heard
Oldest Brother: Justin Wayne Brown (Silver Star and Bronze Star Recipient)
Stepmother: Lillian Brown
Father: James Clarence Brown, Sr.

# CHAPTER 1

# The Leaving from the South

All things in life must change, and at five-years-old, I remember seeing a cross burning in the front yard by the water well out of the huge picture window in our front living room. A few days later, everyone in my family was going on a road trip, moving to the beautiful city of Chicago, Illinois in 1963.

It would always make my mother smile when I told her that I remembered when I saw the cross burning in the yard and the snake that was crawling across my brother, Howard, while he was sleeping. Moving from the South was seeing Southern Royalty at its best because my mother knew the late great Dr. Martin Luther King and his wife, Coretta Scott King, very well. We would hear him preach occasionally on Sundays during his tour of Southern Baptist Churches and the Old Grove Baptist Church in Sprott, Alabama that all of my family attended. Leaving the forty acres and a mule behind as it was said to be for a better life in the North.

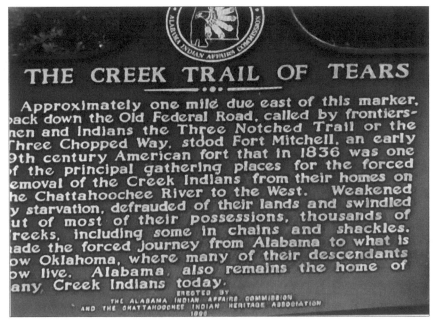

Cherokee and Creek Indian Heritage

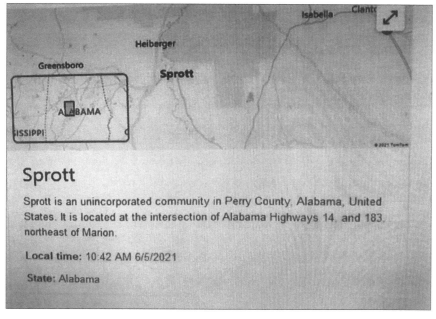

Birthplace: Sprott, Alabama

Mother Mrs. Annie Ruth Heard Brown, Aunt Thelma, Bolling, and Aunt Ray

I can recount the stories my grandmother would tell me about how I got my name. My grandmother, Lela Heard, was a full-blooded Cherokee Indian who chewed tobacco and dipped snuff. My grandfather, Bolling Senior, got his name from Clyde Bolling, the previous owner of the land that I was born on.

Then the name was given to my late Uncle Bolling Heard who fought in World War II, where he was killed not in battle, but at a juke joint party in the backwoods of Alabama. To this day, no one knows what exactly happened during that dice game or who stabbed him in the back with a knife. Even though my dad was also there and saw the whole incident, he never once talked about it, making everyone think that he knew more than what was being told.

Then I, Bolling Heard Brown III, was born on September 28, 1958; the one telling the true story of my great Southern Royalty family. The essence of Sothern Royalty is being blessed by God with all the great spiritual teachings and ethics of all the great ancestors of the Southern

United States of America past and present. A family that is driven by God to do the right things in life. The essence of Southern Royalty is to be noted for hard work and faith in each other. God has put my family as an example for others in the South to follow--to show everyone that you must believe in God first and must always have faith.

I can always remember my mother and grandmother telling me that I was named Bolling for a reason: to carry the family name and its traditions as far as I could and to be that special person that I am. I was taught some of the Biblical secrets, including to always work hard and learn as much as possible from everyone and the secrets that always helped a person overcome anything with faith, prayer, and willingness to listen and learn. If you always treated people the way you wanted to be treated, life would open doors that you never could imagine were possible. We were all taught to pray daily and how to honor the Ten Commandments. I always talked about seeing things before they happened.

This is the Southern Royalty gift that I had, and my mother and grandmother told me that by helping others I would help myself to be whatever I wanted in life. It took me many years to perfect this gift, and I could never tell anyone about it. Having the knowledge to see or know what was going to happen before it happened had its advantages and disadvantages. Meaning that you would be disciplined if you did anything that was not consistent with the teachings of God.

My family finally arrived in Chicago and settled on the west side of town, where our family members, one by one, became legendary. My mother was always the example for everyone to follow in her strict religious ways in how she raised everyone. We were made not to use profanity, to not bare false witness, and to never steal. Basically, she raised us all from the verses of the Ten Commandments. My oldest brother became a millionaire, and my mother was noted as one of the best cooks on the westside of Chicago. Everyone for miles would always come by our house on Sundays after church to buy my mother's dinners (even though she would feed them for free). My other brother, Howard, or, known to all today as Reverend Howard Brown, was noted to be one of the biggest street entrepreneurs in all of the westside of Chicago.

My dad was one of the hardest working men I will ever know, who, with my mother, raised eleven children during the civil rights movement when the country was more divided than ever. He noticed all other families were getting federal or state financial aid assistance. My dad owned a construction company/maintenance cleaning and building repair business, and he owned several apartment complexes on the westside of Chicago. On a normal day he would work from sunrise to sunset, which was twelve to sixteen hours, six or seven days a week. That depended on what needed to be done, like an emergency or something that could wait to the next business day.

Then the family became Southern Royalty when a family member became a millionaire by winning the Illinois State Lottery for over one million dollars in the late 70's. This made almost everyone's dreams come true, but it also brought a lot of jealousy and grief to the Brown, Heard, and Foster family members. It was very hard for everyone. Yet bills got paid now, and no one had to worry about wearing hand me down clothes from one sibling to the other. My mother and sisters were able to dress nice and get the things that they always wanted for themselves.

I was reaching my teenage years and had a secret dream of playing professional basketball. I was truly naturally talented with one of the sweetest jump shots in the city of Chicago. This kept me out of the gangs, from using drugs, and from hanging out with the wrong crowd of people. After playing in a summer league basketball tournament at the Martin Luther King Jr. boys and girls club, I won the MVP, "Most Valuable Player," award for that summer, getting a trophy that was at least four feet tall as my reward for averaging over twenty points a game and ten rebounds a game that summer. This made me fall in love with the game of basketball forever.

I played for the John Marshal High School Commandos and for Coach Luther Bedford who taught me and all of his players how to be men--good people on and off the court. We were the original hoop dreamers because we all dreamed of using basketball to get us out of the ghettos of westside of Chicago, away from the drugs, pimping, pandering, gangs, and people just plain dying for useless reasons.

After finishing high school, I received a four-year basketball scholarship to Eureka College in the southern part of the state of Illinois. I was heavily recruited by Eureka and other colleges in the surrounding states: Indiana, Ohio, Wisconsin, and many others. I had to report to summer basketball camp in early August to complete my enrollment for my first year of college. I still give thanks to my high school coach, Luther Bedford, who always made me work harder than I thought I could.

I never will forget the day when I told my family that I was going to college on a four-year college basketball scholarship. My dad was the first person to ask me who was going to pay for all my college expenses. I proudly picked up the daily newspaper that he had on the coffee table, *The Chicago Daily Defender*, turned to the sports page, and showed him a big article that was written about me having one of the biggest games of my high school career. He then knew that I had enough talent to go to college without him, my mother, or my stepmother worrying about who was going to pay for me to get a college education.

But after one year passed, I decided to try a different route to pursue my professional basketball dreams. The cold weather helped with my decision--it was unbearable. Being the coldest winter in Illinois state history, I had to find a way out, so I prayed for God to hear my prayers and show me a better way.

# CHAPTER 2

# Finding My Purpose

Iwas recruited by the military during my first year in college and saw that this could be another way to get out of the cold weather and move toward better life.

Leaving Chicago after eighteen years of cold weather and a strict religious upbringing was more than enough for me to handle. I had seen visions of a better life in other places of the world than the west side of Chicago where I learned survival skills from my brothers and sisters, my basketball coach, and my mother and father. Where I learned to always strive for the best and work hard to be the best.

I joined the United States Marine Corps in the summer of 1977. After boot camp in San Diego, California, I returned home and resumed my college studies until the worst winter in Chicago history happened. That winter was what pushed me over the edge to decide on leaving for good by going on active duty to the Marine Corps base at Camp Pendleton in California. When your tears freeze on your face and icicles hang from your nose, that's too cold for me.

After an illustrious fourteen-year military career, I was medically retired for injuries suffered while on active duty. I fell into a semi-depression after being discharged from the military because I suffered from PTSD and did not know what it was that made me drink alcohol and do other illegal substances. I'd seen people vomiting from fear and hurting themselves on purpose so that they could go home or to be sent to the nearest hospital. They were scared. I still have nightmares of the dark, hot summer nights in the jungles where everything that could possibly kill you was there--snakes, alligators, vampire bats, and the enemy that you feared most of all. Some of the young men in my squad couldn't sleep because they just wanted to go home. Praying to God is what got me home all in one peace. Even though we were told we was on a training mission in the country of Panama, Suez canal zone.

Finally, I went back to the teachings of my grandmother and mother; I reached deep inside my mind and found the inner peace that God speaks and had it guide me to a better life. I asked Him to help me whenever I needed to be put back on track. Thanks to my sister, Cynthia, who told me how I was screwing up, I used my Southern Royalty skills to escalate myself to a new chapter in my life..

Basketball was the one skill that I still was practicing at a very high level and was on the brink of signing a professional contract. I then continued to play for the NBA Seattle Supersonics in the D-League system with dreams and hopes of moving to their A-League team, the Spokane Washington Thunderbirds. However, training was very difficult to do, as well as getting good workouts or playing with good competition, while having a family to provide for.

While still chasing my dream of playing professional basketball, another opportunity came about for a spot in a movie called *White Men Can't Jump*. Unfortunately, I was not informed in time for the initial interviews. One of the actors in the movie, a Mr. Lewis Price formerly of the Temptations, was selected for a cameo part in the movie. This really bothered me because Lewis and I went to the same high school, he graduated four years ahead of me and was on the same team during pickup workout games at the Sears YMCA on the west side of Chicago. While playing under Coach Luther Bedford at John Marshall High School I worked out against Lewis to escalate my game to the pro level and played against Chicago Bulls all-star forward Mickey Johnson and others when I was only sixteen years old. I knew this was an opportunity that I had missed.

It worked out, though. By the next week, I had made the front cover of the sports page in the city of Oceanside newspaper. This was sort of a consolation prize for me who just kept going on to try and achieve my place in stardom. After playing in an all-star basketball game at Los Angeles High School, I helped raise over $100,000 for charity organizations. My contributions went to a homeless shelter called "Brother Benos's" in Oceanside, California and the Boys & Girls Club of Oceanside in California..

I then moved my family to beautiful Las Vegas, Nevada where my first cousin, Mrs. Lavern Patton, and her family lived. She had always been the matriarch for the Heard and Brown families respectively. I needed a change from California because things in Oceanside were not getting any better for me and my family. I wanted to strive for better opportunities in beautiful Las Vegas, Nevada. We stayed in Las Vegas for only a couple of years because the heat and the lifestyle there was too much for my family and I to bear. The constant parties, drinking, gambling, lawlessness, and underworld activities will not be mentioned to protect the innocence of myself, my family, and others..

So, I moved my family back to Oceanside, California. Using my military training, I got into the security and law enforcement industry where my credentials were unbelievably superb.

I completed a great fourteen-year career in the United States Marine Corps where I was taught things that I can't, or are very hard to, explain to anyone. I was a weapons expert and range instructor, and I trained with the Navy Seals in San Diego. I then obtained a black belt in karate and a brown belt in aikido, and advanced office administration. Basically, I was taught, and did not realize at the time, methods of how to exterminate or get rid of people or problems.

I also acquired the credentials of a Certified Rappel Master, a Cold-Weather War Expert, a Jungle Warfare Expert, and I graduated from the Federal Law Enforcement in Glynco, Georgia for Federal Corrections Officers in the upper ten percent of my graduating class of 1990, with a GPA 0f 94.6 percent. This is the same academy that the U.S. Marshalls, U.S. Border Patrol, and Alcohol Tobacco Firearms (ATF) of the United States Federal Justice Department all attend for their certification training.

I learned and obtained skills and knowledge that always benefitted me and my family if used the right way. If I were looking for a word to describe myself at that period in my life, it would be "badass," and that is why I got into the security industry, and, to this present day, have an illustrious and beautiful career. This helped me to raise my family of two sons, Jacoby and Joshua, and two daughters, Aisha and Tysheena. My children were one of the major reasons why I worked so hard daily, often putting in seventy to eighty hours every week.

I know now that being trained by the best in the world, I can't hide or hold these experiences to myself. That would be total selfishness. My career, as of now, is as a First Responder Captain / Account Manager / Site Supervisor / Post Commander all rolled into one. I complete another four days a week in a different roll with another security based company as well. If you want something in life, you better work for it, because no one is going to give you anything.

That is the hard work ethic I have learned over the years from my mother, father, coaches, the military, and Southern Royalty: to always try and be the best at everything I do, no matter what. Still to this day, I have minor PTSD and other physical injuries I suffered while on active duty in the Marine Corps. So I just pray and enjoy the company of my beautiful wife and work very hard to keep my mind going in the right directions. I have to attend bi-weekly therapy and stimulating acupuncture heat and massage treatments and take pain medications as needed for my back and sciatica nerve pains. I have a psychiatrist to help me stay focused on not falling back into my PTSD moods again. This works great for me on a daily basis, and these treatments have given me the courage to write this book.

Bolling and Police Chief Ms. Nancy Zimmerman of San Diego, California

# CHAPTER 3

# Waunience Cole Brown Story

God blessed me with a miracle: my wife, Waunience Cole Brown. It all started with meeting the love of my life and, at the time I met her, I did not know that we would forever be attached.

We were attending summer school at Whitney Young High School on the southwest side of Chicago. I had to take a college precatory course before honoring my four year basketball scholarship to Eureka College.

We were sitting in class doing morning roll call for the daily student attendance when, from across the room, she gave me a glancing look and the prettiest smile I had ever seen. I was in love and did not even know it. We went on our first date about a week later, and our emotions at eighteen-years-old were intense; we were all over each other.

After one year passed, I joined the United States Marine Corps Reserves. It was too cold in the state of Illinois, and I needed a way to get to a better life than what I had. I already had a great life, but I wanted more--I wanted to play professional basketball and make a lot of money to take care of my future family and my mother and father.

My mother and stepmother were the two people I credit all of my success to because they always said to me "be somebody." They told me not to be like everyone else because it was something special that I had, and that was why I was named Bolling Heard Brown III. I had all that it took to make my family proud. That's the Southern Royalty I inherited from my family's teachings that I received growing up. It was ingrained into me to be the best I could be no matter what. With my Indian blood, I always knew about things before they happened. What a blessing to have and a burden to carry, and no one ever knew but my mother, grandmother, and the elderly members of the family.

Oldest Son: Jacoby Lazar Holmes Brown
Wife: Waunience Cole Brown
Author: Bolling Heard Brown III

CEO, CFO, caretaker, wife, and philanthropist. Mrs. Waunience Cole Brown, who is truly the foundation of Bolling Heard Brown III and the essence of Southern Royalty.

Prayer is the true meaning of Southern Royalty, and the
strength of the Brown family.

NBA Coach Mike Brown and Bolling getting a
coffee in San Diego, California

Bolling visited at work by three-time NBA Champion
Shawn Livingston of the Golden States Warriors

Bolling visited by NBA player Gordon Hayward

Bolling and wife Waunience at the George Floyd Memorial in Minneapolis, Minnesota, acknowledging that the year of 2020 showed everyone that Black Lives Matter.

Honoring sister-in-law Elsie Jean Cole,
and everyone who loved her very much

Bolling and San Diego Police Chief

Son: Joshua
Daughters: Tysheena and Aisha
Celebrating another Southern Royalty birthday

Bolling and Waunience at the George Floyd memorial in Minneapolis, Minnesota. This site changed the world and brought a different perspective to all people. No matter what color, creed, or religion, God brought all people closer together during this year of 2020. Also, the COVID-19 pandemic made a lot of people during this year rethink their priorities because 600,000 people died from the COVID-19 virus that year.

# CHAPTER 4

# Keeping the Faith

I carved out a very good life in Oceanside, California for about twenty years before I moved inland about twenty miles to the beautiful city of Escondido.

In 2013, I knew that after years of just getting by, paying bills, and raising kids was not enough for what dreams were still haunting me. Being Southern Royalty, I was destined to be or do something great for myself and my family.

One day in 2014, after being on my knees praying to the heavenly Father to just give me a sign of what I should do next, it happened.

I was looking for a restaurant due to an idea my brother and I were talking about: a fast-food place that was going to be called "Ruth's Place" with a Chicago-style, southern flavored eatery with all the trimmings. I was looking up ideas on the internet for Chicago-style food and marketing ideas, when Lord behold, I typed in a phone number for a Ms. Waunience Cole. I wanted to see if she was still alive or even still living in Chicago. A number popped up which was the same number she had had thirty-five years ago.

I called the number, and her mother answered the phone. I asked if that was the number where Waunience Cole lived, and her mother said yes. She said that Waunience was not there, but she would get her the message that I called. I didn't know at the time that her mother was suffering from a bad case of dementia and old age. She wrote my phone number down, and Waunience called me about one week later.

Waiting on her to call was God's will because I fell instantly in love with her again the first time I heard her voice after thirty-five years. It was a miracle that I had been blessed with from God. I never thought I would ever talk to Waunience again. I decided to make a trip to Chicago to meet Waunience. She was waiting at the airport to pick me up.

Waunience

My first thoughts were that she was going to be old, out of shape, wrinkled, or something truly unwaning. However, when I saw her through the window waiting near her car, she was so beautiful. I was speechless while we drove to the Best Western hotel near the airport.

We were married on my birthday, September 28, 2016, in Las Vegas, Nevada, with my brother Zackary as my best man and all of my children present as witnesses.

This was one of the best things that ever happened to me in my life, besides being born. I constantly say that God brought us back together because that is the Southern Royalty way of life.

Mother Mrs. Annie Ruth Heard Brown

Mother

My mother, Mrs. Annie Ruth Heard Brown, who is the total inspiration of this autobiography, and is who made me understand that God is the ultimate strength in achieving greatness and prosperity and taught me how to embrace the world in His eyes and no one else's. She also taught me how to embrace His name and that He was Southern Royalty. That's why I was named Bolling Heard Brown III. To carry the name of three generations is not an easy task. I was taught by the best of the best to always get it right, then share that with others so that the world can be a better place for all humanity.

# CHAPTER 5

# It's All About Family

Mrs. Waunience Cole Brown

The Essence of Southern Royalty: Family
Bolling, Zackary, Anthony, Elizabeth, Joseph,
and Cynthia

Southern Royalty family
at sister Jean's birthday party.
The Brown Family, Southern Royalty
From left to right: Bolling, Zachary, Elizabeth, Anthony,
Joseph, and Cynthia

My brother, Reverend Howard Brown, who taught me how to pray and be a good man and person. His tutelage was priceless in my adolescent years and still is as an adult today. I will always seek knowledge from my brother.

Bolling and Waunience at home in beautiful San Diego, California

# CHAPTER 6

# Never Forget Where You Come From

Remembering the Southern Royalty Gift that I was given showed me that people of color who were suffering from abuse and prejudice would soon find peace. I saw a vision of me and my children doing great things together. That is how Waunience came back into my life. I knew this was going to happen because God took over my thoughts and guided me to her (as well as her to me). It's magical, to say the least.

At the George Floyd memorial, we gave prayer and thanks to see God had blessed the ground where George Floyd was killed. I felt the pain in the neighborhood and on the street where he was killed. I could feel a strong sense of euphoria knowing that the suffering had come to an end. I finished taking a few more pictures with my wife then departed that memorial ground with tears in my eyes.

Sugg Knight and Bolling acknowledging their blessings

Mayor Terry Johnson, the first Black Mayor in San Diego North County history, pictured with Bolling in Oceanside, California. A true blessing was bestowed upon Bolling in meeting Mr. Terry Johnson, as his personal bodyguard and then, later, as a good true friend.

Hands of Prayer

Always remember to say your prayers and give thanks daily, and never forget that there is a higher power. God has blessed me with so much. He's given me beautiful children and life experiences that would make the average person give up. Yet, keeping the faith of where I come from and learning the Cherokee and Creek Indians way of life from my mother, father, and the elders of the family has given me a foresight into the future.

Having the knowledge to see things before they happen has its advantages and disadvantages. So to all of my sisters, Gloria, Cynthia, Elizabeth, and Gwendolyn, and my brothers, Justin, James, Howard, Anthony, Joseph, and Zachary; to my uncles and aunts and grandparents; to my first cousins, Lavern, Clara, Shirley, Mira, Daisey, Dennis, Oretha, Margarete, Dale, Bobby, Alphonso, Danny, Ronnie, and too many others to count or mention--know that I am always thinking of you in my heart.

I love you all for making me understand the gift from God that I was given, which makes us all who we are today: Southern Royalty. Of the world that God has created for us all to cherish: respect, prosper, love, work hard, and never forget that we are all Southern Royalty. I always tell everyone I meet on a daily basis, "If you want everlasting happiness, peace, and love in your life, you must remember the Ten Commandments and the Serenity Prayer." That is the Southern Royalty way of life that I was taught. It has made me remarkably successful, happy, and blessed throughout my life.

CHAPTER 7

# Teachings of the Essence of Southern Royalty

———— ✳ ————

Tablet of the Ten Commandments

Tablet of the Ten Commandments (6-10)

These Commandments are the teachings that I was taught daily by my mother, father, aunts, uncles, grandparents, and cousins, who were all an enormous influence for me to understand that I was Southern Royalty.

Bolling and wife Waunience on San Diego harbor
Bolling Heard Brown III and Waunience Cole Brown on San Diego Harbor

Mother Mrs. Annie Ruth Heard Brown

Mother

Aunt Elmira. Teacher of the essence
of Southern Royalty.

Serenity Prayer

This prayer is what Bolling lives by every day. He shares it with everyone he meets to give them the understanding that, if it's in God's Hands, everything will be alright.

# CHAPTER 8

# Doing God's Work

Always trying your best at everything you do is very hard, I know. But if you put that trust in God Almighty, you will immediately see a difference in everything you do. What you say, how you talk, and everything you touch will be significantly different for the better.

Always have faith, and never give up. I am so lucky and blessed to have a family of Southern Royalty as I do, and many other families should have this as well. Just remember the Ten Commandments and the Serenity Prayer. These will always keep you on path to greatness and reinforce you as a child of God. When I did not have anyone to talk to, I just got on my knees and reminded God of our personal, special relationship and asked him to just show me a better way of life. I gave Him all of my thoughts and ideas to handle because I was not able to go forward anymore. By keeping faith and believing in yourself, anything can be accomplished. God put my beautiful wife, Waunience, back into my life when I needed her the most. The women in my life at that time were not who I wanted to spend my life with forever. That was God's miracle to me that will forever keep me grateful and humble.

Southern royalty logo.

Mother Mrs. Annie Ruth Heard Brown, Aunt Thelma,
Bolling Heard Brown III, and Aunt Ray, Aunt Elmira.
These are the beautiful ladies who taught me the essence of Southern Royalty.

# Written By:
# Bolling Heard Brown III

In loving memory of my mother, Mrs. Annie Ruth Heard Brown, and father, Mr. James Clarence Brown Sr. To my brothers and sisters, aunts, cousins, and grandparents. To God, who has given me the ultimate gift of being His son with an instrument to share His blessings worldwide: being the essence of Southern Royalty.

Author Mr. Bolling Heard Brown III and Mrs. Waunience Cole Brown,
who is always also the essence of Southern Royalty.

CPSIA information can be obtained
at www.ICGtesting.com
Printed in the USA
LVHW070415030322
712196LV00002BA/11